The JU

MEAU DOLL

Margaret Whitton

Associate Curator, Dolls
The Margaret Woodbury Strong Museum
Rochester, New York

Photographs by
J. Kent Campbell

Dover Publications, Inc., New York
in association with
The Margaret Woodbury Strong Museum

Acknowledgments

I should like to thank those individuals and organizations who so willingly offered me their assistance and support in the writing of this book.

My gratitude is extended to Chuck Bayles of Vistec Graphics Ltd.; Monica Burkhardt of the Musée des Arts Décoratifs, Paris; J. Kent Campbell, my photographer; Dorothy and Jane Coleman, authors of *The Collector's Book of Dolls' Clothes* and *The Collector's Encyclopedia of Dolls;* Mary Hillier of Redhill, England; Douglas B. Remington, who translated the Tissandier article; Mary Kay Ingenthron, public relations director of the Margaret Woodbury Strong Museum; Rita Weiss, my editor, and the many individual members of the United Federation of Doll Collectors and the Doll Collectors of America.

M. W.

Published in Canada by General Publishing Company, Ltd., 30 Lesmill Road, Don Mills, Toronto, Ontario.

Published in the United Kingdom by Constable and Company, Ltd., 10 Orange Street, London WC2H 7EG.

The Jumeau Doll is a new work, first published by Dover Publications, Inc., in 1980.

Book design by Carol Belanger Grafton

International Standard Book Number: 0-486-23954-3
Library of Congress Catalog Card Number: 80-65737

Manufactured in the United States of America
Dover Publications, Inc.
180 Varick Street
New York, N.Y. 10014

Introduction

The fascination with dolls seems to be a universal human trait that knows no boundaries of age, culture or sex. A doll may fulfill many different roles—a religious symbol, a purveyor of the latest fashions—but it is first and foremost a plaything to be loved and enjoyed by generations of children. The enchantment with dolls manifests itself in many ways, not the least of which is the joy of collecting antique ones. Among the dolls most sought after by collectors are those manufactured in France by the Jumeau factory during the nineteenth and early part of the twentieth century. This book is a pictorial history of those dolls.

I have tried to show in this book the various types of dolls made during the company's long history as well as give some indication of the important points of identification. All of the dolls shown in this book come from the collection in the Margaret Woodbury Strong Museum in Rochester, New York. It is my hope that this volume will aid those who are avid collectors as well as those who are just beginning to collect and also be of interest to those who simply love beautiful dolls.

Pierre François Jumeau founded his doll company in 1842. In the early years, Jumeau apparently had a partner named Belton. Their names appear together in Paris city directories from 1842 to 1846, and the firm of Jumeau and Belton exhibited dolls at the Paris Exposition of 1844, receiving honorable mention for their work. After 1846, Belton is no longer mentioned, and Pierre Jumeau's name appears alone in the 1848 directory where his address is listed as 18, Rue Mauconseil, Paris.

By the middle of the nineteenth century doll making had become a vital and far-reaching industry in Europe. Many of the heads Jumeau used came from Germany; the wax shoulder heads from England; the character heads and composition bodies from Paris. Even the manufacture of stockings, shoes, hats, feet, hands and wigs had become a big industry. (At the time of the 1849 Paris Exposition, Jumeau was employing 65 sewers, leather workers, dressers and hat trimmers who were paid by the job.) Pierre Jumeau was determined to make France the center of the world's doll industry.

In 1849 Jumeau won a Bronze Medal at the Paris Exposition. The jury report from the Exposition states in part, "The kid (body) doll has proven Paris to have such superior workmanship, taste and low price that it is exported all over the world; it need never fear competition. This fact makes Pierre Jumeau's Exposition exhibit particularly in-teresting: his gross income is 120,000 francs, most of his goods are exported, and the goods are known in China." The report adds that "Mr. Jumeau obviously has just about reached the limit of low-priced goods; at the same time, he is one who has succeeded in making queens, marquises, and character dolls."

Jumeau also gained recognition for dolls' layettes and trousseaus which sold wholesale from as little as 12 francs a dozen up to as much as 150 francs a piece. According to the same jury report, the trousseaus were composed of the doll and nine pieces of clothing. The best-selling item at the exposition was the trousseau-layette which sold for 4 francs 50 centimes for a box that included a 24" doll with a 26-piece wardrobe.

"The manufacture is truly remarkable," the report concluded. "The clothed doll is not only a plaything, but often provides a foreigner with a model of our fashions and has become, in recent years, the indispensable shipment item of our latest innovations to the Americas and the Indies."

At the first International Exhibition, organized and sponsored by Prince Albert, Queen Victoria's consort, in London in 1851, Jumeau was awarded a First Place Medal. The jury for this exhibition made the following comment about Jumeau's exhibit: "The dolls on which these dresses are displayed present no point worthy of commendation, but the dresses themselves are very beautiful." By 1867, however, Jumeau received a Silver Medal at the Paris Exhibition, and for the first time mention was made of the dolls' heads.

At the Vienna Exhibition in 1873, Jumeau again won plaudits for his work. He was awarded the Medal of Progress and a Gold Medal. The French report of this exhibition gives a lengthy account of his work. It states, in part, "Mr. Jumeau of Paris, the first and most important dollmaking house, has freed us from our former obligation to have the foreigner furnish us with porcelain doll heads. Mr. Jumeau has established at Montreuil, near Paris, a factory where he makes doll heads of glazed porcelain with the greatest perfection. He has surpassed in beauty the products that we used to buy from Saxony."

The Philadelphia Exposition of 1876 lists Pierre Jumeau as the winner of a Gold Medal for his display of dolls' heads and bodies: "A fine collection, dressed in a most fashionable style; heads of the finest imitation (life-like), superior taste and excellent workmanship in mechanical construction."

Much of what we know today about the early growth of the Jumeau company comes from listings for Pierre Jumeau in the Paris City Directory located in the library of

Advertising card promoting the Jumeau doll and emphasizing the awards that Pierre Jumeau won in 1851, 1855 and 1867. The two beautifully costumed dolls shown appear to be fashion dolls.

the Paris Chamber of Commerce. Here are some selected listings for the years in which new innovations were introduced.

1859 Jumeau: Maker of nude dolls in kid or dressed dolls of all kinds; trousseaus; dolls with porcelain heads. Medal 1849, 1851 and 1855.

1861 Jumeau: Jointed (probably kid bodies) dolls with porcelain heads; talking dolls. Exposition.

1865 Jumeau: Maker of all kinds of kid dolls, nude or dressed; dresses for jointed dolls or sculptured dolls with porcelain heads; talking dolls. Award of medals in London and Paris. 18, Rue Mauconseil.

1867 Same entry as for 1865 but the address now is 8, Rue d'Anjou-Marais.

1871 Jumeau: Maker of all kinds of dolls, nude or dressed; trousseaus; jointed dolls, sculptured dolls; porcelain heads; talking baby dolls. Winner of medal in London and Paris, 1867. 8, Rue d'Anjou-Marais.

1873 Jumeau: Same entry as for 1871 except for the addition "at Montreuil-sous-Bois."

1876 Jumeau: Same entry as for 1873 with the addition "Workshop at Montreuil-sous-Bois."

1877 Jumeau: 8, Rue d'Anjou-Marais. Maker of all kinds of dolls. Kid dolls, stiff or bendable; jointed dolls in sculptured wood; linen or silk (clothing) dolls conforming with the latest Paris fashions. Dolls' trousseaus and linens. Jumeau unbreakable dolls. [This no doubt refers to the ball-jointed composition bodies, not the heads—M.W.] Special line in making of porcelain heads. Workshops at Montreuil-sous-Bois. Winner of first prizes at all exhibitions; latest of which was at Philadelphia.

During Pierre Jumeau's control of the company little attempt was made to advertise the Jumeau doll. Three magazines that were specifically directed at young girls— *La Poupée*, *Gazette de la Poupée* and *La Poupée Modèle*—occasionally printed patterns to fit dolls made by French manufacturers such as Jumeau. A print appearing in *La Poupée* in 1864 did show two Jumeau dolls. The dolls resemble what we today call fashion dolls and probably had bisque heads with kid bodies. (These fashion dolls served a two-fold purpose. They were couriers of fashion as well as playthings, their primary function.) The print is captioned "Poupées et Costumes de la Maison Jumeau, Rue Mauconseil, 18." (Dolls and costumes from the firm of Jumeau. . . .)

Pierre Jumeau had planned to have his oldest son, George, take over the business upon his retirement. However, George died very suddenly, and when Pierre retired in 1877 or 1878, the second son, Emile Jumeau, took over as head of the company.

Emile Jumeau had studied to be an architect, never dreaming that his father's business would one day be his. When he did take over, he conducted the business with the same zest and determination as had his father in an attempt to make France the world leader in the doll industry. A born promoter, his inventions, advertising schemes and exaggerated claims were all directed toward this goal. Under his management the company reached its zenith, and during the next 20 years the Jumeau company became one of the leading doll manufacturing concerns in the world. In 1886 Emile was named by France as a Chevalier de la Légion d'Honneur in recognition of his achievements. His listings in the Paris City Directory tell the story of the development of the company:

The Jumeau doll factory, 1878.

1878   Jumeau, E.: Kid dolls stiff or bendable. Jointed wooden dolls. Linen or silk dolls [probably means clothing] of finest quality and conforming with the latest fashions. Perfect workmanship. Jumeau unbreakable dolls. Special line in making of porcelain heads. Workshops at Montreuil. Winner of first prizes at all exhibitions, latest of which is Philadelphia. Suppliers to shops selling latest novelties.

1879   Jumeau, Emile: Gold medal, Paris 1878. Maker of dolls in kid or jointed wood. Unbreakable *Bébé* dolls. Unique models. Linen or silk dolls of finest quality and conforming with the latest fashions.

1882   Jumeau, Emile: 85,000 Jumeau jointed composition dolls were sold in 1881. Jumeau *Bébé* dolls. Nos. 9 to 16 have paperweight eyes and applied ears; they wear a necklace of Paris pearls to hide the neck joint, and have a comb in their hair. *Bébé* dolls in kid. These *Bébé* dolls are made exactly like an ordinary doll, have all its defects and are not recommended by my firm, which makes them only on

Emile Jumeau.

precise order. [It is interesting that he would bother to advertise this doll even though not recommending it—*M.W.*]

1884   Jumeau, Emile: Same entry as for 1882 with one addition: "Jumeau talking *Bébé* dolls, a new creation."

1885   Jumeau, Emile: Much the same as for 1884, but the following additions: "The Jumeau unbreakable *Bébé* dolls. All carry the maker's name. First marketed in 1879. 110,000 were sold in 1883."

One of the first things Emile Jumeau did upon taking command of the company was to completely rebuild the old walled Jumeau factory in Montreuil. He spent large sums of money transforming the factory into an imposing, magnificent structure. Three buildings formed the three sides of a long parallelogram with a huge clock tower dominating the building at the farthest end. An impressive gate served as the front entrance of the walled enclosure. On either side of the gate stood large panels with huge carved lettering which proclaimed: "Manufacture Bébé Jumeau, Medaille d'Or 1878" (Bébé Jumeau Factory, Gold Medal, 1878).

In succeeding years Emile Jumeau became more and more successful, employing approximately 50 people in the factory, most of them women. A brochure describing a visit to the factory states, "Women's work, as is well known, is very badly paid. Monsieur Jumeau has reacted against this bad habit, the cause of so many fallen women, alas! He has given himself the unrewarding task of employing as many women as possible in his factory. He pays them a very good salary. Owing to the work being well paid, one cannot accuse Monsieur Jumeau of having thought to find cheap labor by employing mostly women." Many collectors and researchers feel that Jumeau wrote and distributed the brochure himself as a means of advertising his company.

Emile Jumeau is best known for his "Bébés," which he claimed to have invented. For years the emphasis in doll manufacturing had been on the mature "lady type" with the bisque head and kid body, shaped to accent the beautiful French fashions of the time. Jumeau began to produce dolls in a child-like form as well as the fashion ladies. The Bébés had bisque heads with composition- or wood-jointed bodies held together by elastic. The heads could be turned from side to side and the bodies were flexible at the joints, enabling a child to put the Bébé into different positions. The composition for the bodies consisted of various materials—paper, wood chips, etc.—molded together to form the different parts of the body.

Much of the charm of the Jumeau dolls lay in their elaborate underclothing, dresses, hats, shoes and jewelry; and their wardrobes and accessories played an important part in the success of the company. Some of the clothing was made at the factory in Montreuil, especially the shoes, socks and plain underclothing or chemises. Often the dolls were shipped in their boxes clad only in this clothing because many of the buyers enjoyed choosing their own costumes and dressing their own dolls. A large number of the Bébés, however, were sent to the Jumeau shop on the Rue Pastourelle where Madame Jumeau provided the very finest wardrobes for the dolls. Approximately 50 people were employed in this shop with Madame Jumeau herself making the decisions about patterns or designs for the clothing. Besides those working at the shop, there were some 200 women, called "outside workers," who sewed at home and were paid by the number of pieces they created.

Besides being an astute businessman and promoter, Emile Jumeau was also an inventor. A number of patents were issued to him, most of which dealt with the eye mechanism of the doll. In 1885 he invented a method for making the eyelids close over the eyeballs (see page 26). In 1886 he received a patent for making a doll of "unbreakable" material. Another patent was obtained in 1887 for sleeping eyes which included eyelashes, giving the doll a more lifelike appearance.

Unlike his father, Emile Jumeau believed strongly in the power of advertising, and he employed a number of clever ideas to publicize his dolls. Many of his promotions were devised to denigrate the German doll manufacturers because of Jumeau's determination to make France number one in the doll industry. One of the most clever of these advertising devices is the one pictured on page 64. It is a game called "Grand Game of Jumeau's Doll 1889," specifically designed for the American market. The game is a sizeable sheet, 27" x 17", printed in bright colors on thin paper so that it could be wrapped around a doll when the doll was shipped to the United States. The Eiffel Tower appears in the foreground with the Jumeau walled factory at Montreuil and the Statue of Liberty in the distance. At the right hand of the sheet there is a doll holding the American flag and at the left a doll holding the French flag. There are 63 numbers on the Eiffel Tower with some numbers containing pictures of German dolls. The idea of the game is not to fall on the numbers representing German dolls. The first player to reach 63 wins the game. The game is dedicated to young Americans and states, "The Jumeau doll brings good luck, we therefore hope young players may not be so unfortunate as to be assigned places where there are German dolls." Besides serving as an advertising scheme for Jumeau dolls, the game commemorated the opening of the Eiffel Tower, designed for the Exposition of 1889 by Alexandre Gustave Eiffel.

Page 63 shows two of the small illustrated booklets which Jumeau often packed with his dolls, another of his advertising schemes. *Purchase Me Young Lady* is a story written as if the doll herself were talking to a small child, telling the child where she was born and that she was created by Emile Jumeau. The doll goes into detail about the great effort made by Jumeau to create a perfect Bébé: "Dear man! How rewarded now for all his trouble. From morning to night his warehouse is full of customers: yet indeed, merchants, buyers, commission agents from the five parts of the world come to vie with each other in order to secure his unbreakable dolls. Such as you see me, I carried this great gold medal at the Universal Exhibition in 1878 amid general applause and I may say it was richly deserved."

In another booklet entitled *Letter of a Jumeau Baby to Her Little Mother*, the doll explains how delighted she is to have this little girl as her new mother. She tells how careful Jumeau is to have all of his dolls leave the factory in perfect condition. Any that are not perfect are to be destroyed. The booklet relates Emile Jumeau's reaction to an imperfect doll: "Destroy immediately this trash. What an insult for a well-born baby's self respect. It is good only for those frightful German babies (dolls). They are ugly and ridiculous enough, these German babies, with their stupid faces of waxed cardboard, their goggle eyes and their frail bodies stuffed with hemp threads." The letter ends with: "P.S. If after some too violent a shock, my head should happen to break, do not weep. Go find my father, Mr. Jumeau, clever doll surgeon that he is, he will put another one on me and I will not be any worse for it afterward."

Jumeau dolls were advertised in the catalogs of several French department stores such as La Samaritaine, Louvre, Bon Marché, Printemps and Grand Bazar de l'Hôtel-de-Ville. Occasionally dolls were created by Jumeau especially for these stores. Two such dolls were the Bébé Samaritaine and the Bébé Louvre. The dolls made for the Louvre store are believed to be those with the bisque heads incised with the letters "B.L." (see page 66).

The Jumeau name became so well known that other advertisers started to profit from its fame. In October, 1888, the *Youth's Companion*, an American juvenile periodical, advertised a doll and patterns for her wardrobe as "Our New Jumeau Pattern Doll, Elena." The doll was given as a premium for a specific number of magazine subscriptions. Only a reading of the fine print revealed that the doll was "made after the celebrated Jumeau model." Apparently they were not using a true Jumeau but a substitute that resembled it.

Emile Jumeau always welcomed publicity and whenever writers were interested in visiting his factory and printing information about the business and manufacture of his dolls, he went out of his way to be helpful.

An anonymous 1885 booklet about the Jumeau company was translated and published by Nina S. Davies in 1957 under the title *The Jumeau Doll Story*. Many collectors and

Our New Jumeau Pattern Doll, Eléna.

Given for one new name, and 25 cts. additional.

Fair Eléna

presents her card, and we take pleasure in introducing her to our young friends, who, we know, will be delighted to welcome her.

As she cannot speak English, she will say a few words in French, which we will translate. "I am a thousand times happy to greet you all. You have been such good friends to my cousins, Reta, Adele and Felice, that I know we shall have delightful times together.   ELÉNA."

The Doll Age is the growing age. It is the age in which habits are formed. With a pretty Doll, habits of industry, of neatness and of order can be established.

As we give with the Doll a set of Paper Patterns, a little girl can soon learn (in an amateur way) the art of dressmaking.

Is there a little girl without a love for Dolls? Whether it be of Wax or Rags, of China or Wood, still her heart yearns toward it, and she delights in tending and caressing it.

To Be Encouraged.

We believe this affection should be increased rather than in the least discouraged. Time spent with Dolls is not time thrown away. We are glad that we are still able, as in the past three years, to offer our girls a Doll well worthy of all the love and care that can be lavished upon it.

The Doll Age is a happy age—there is no doubt about it. Much does a pretty Doll contribute to the happiness of this age. Unfortunate must be the little girl who has never owned a Doll. Children of all nations, whether savage or civilized, take equal delight in this universal toy.

The Kitchen Set and Dishes.

All given for one new name

This Set consists of a nice Stove and Furniture, and about 50 useful Tin Dishes, Tea Kettle, etc., etc. The cut gives you a little idea of the variety. No Rolling Pin goes with this Set. This premium is about double the value of the one given last year for one new name. We give the entire Set for one new name. For sale by us for 90 cts. **Postage and packing, 40 cts.,** when sent as a premium or purchased, or sent by express and charges paid by receiver.

Description.

Our new Doll differs from those previously offered by us. It is made after the celebrated Jumeau model, having the ball and socket joints at the elbows, shoulders, knees and hips, also joint at the neck, so that the head can be turned naturally. It has a beautiful Bisque Head, with "Natural" Eyes and flowing Hair of a most luxuriant growth.

Its Lips and Teeth.

This Doll is unlike others with simply a painted mouth. Its lips are beautifully moulded and slightly parted, showing pearly porcelain teeth which have been naturally inserted. They are charming. The Doll is dressed as seen in the cut, and is 16 inches high.

Paper Patterns.

We also give with this Doll a Set of Paper Patterns, with directions for making her wardrobe. These Patterns will enable a girl to do her own cutting and fitting, and will prove to be a most delightful and instructive occupation.

Given for only one new name, and 25 cts. additional. Price, $1.25. Postage and packing, 65 cts., when sent as a premium or purchased. This Doll is larger and much heavier than any of our former Dolls. This accounts for the heavy postage charges. We suggest that when you order the Doll either as a sale or premium, you request us to send it by express, not paid. In most cases it will cost you less by express than by mail.

FELICE.—We have in stock a quantity of the Doll Felice, offered by us last season. Felice has a Kid Body and Bisque Head.

We still offer her for one new name, and 20 cts. additional. Price, $1. Postage and packing, 40 cts., when sent as a premium or purchased.

Child's Decorated China Tea Set.

No. 72½. 23 Pieces. Given for one new name, and 10 cts. additional.

This is the largest and prettiest Child's imported Tea Set we ever used. Each piece is beautifully hand-painted in colors, with gold lines. The Set consists of 23 pieces— **Tea Pot, Sugar Bowl, Cream Pitcher, 6 Plates and 6 Cups and Saucers.** The Tea Pot is 5 in. high, and other pieces in proportion. All packed in moss in a wooden box. Given for one new name, and 10 cts. additional. Price, $1. **Sent by express, and charges paid by receiver,** when sent as a premium or purchased.

Advertisement from *The Youth's Companion;* the doll offered as a premium is not a true Jumeau but one "made after the celebrated Jumeau model."

researchers feel that Emile Jumeau himself wrote the original brochure, giving a very detailed report of the inner workings of his factory.

Several other works were written about the factory in Montreuil. Gaston Tissandier wrote about his visit in 1888, and this was published in the scientific magazine *La Nature. Pearson's Magazine* printed a story by M. Dinorben Griffith, entitled "A Village of Dollmakers," that described the different departments and procedures in the manufacture of the Jumeau dolls. Léo Claretie in his book *Les Jouets, Histoire Fabrication,* published in Paris in 1898, also wrote about his visit.

All of these accounts agree in many respects. Each author speaks of the various stages: the making of the head molds, the painting rooms, the blowing of the glass eyes, wig making, the assembling of the dolls, and the costuming. Tissandier's article for *La Nature* gives an excellent description not only of the factory but of the entire procedure for making the dolls. The article has been especially translated for this book, and is included here along with the illustrations which appeared in the original article.

Our readers know that we look for curiosities of science in whatever area they may be found, and that children's toys have often offered us the opportunity to study some ingenious mechanisms. Playthings are of no less interest from the industrial point of view than they are from the scientific point of view, as will be seen by this article. Before the visit that we had the opportunity to make to the famous doll factory at Montreuil, near Paris, we failed to suspect the magnitude that could be attained by this very special type of industry. The director and founder of this factory, Mr. Jumeau, whose name is universally known, did us the honor of showing us his establishment with most gracious courtesy, and we express to him here our grateful thanks. We are going to try to impart to our readers our surprise – in fact, our amazement – at seeing such well-organized production.

The doll factory at Montreuil makes only deluxe dolls, with porcelain heads and papier-mâché bodies: it is the largest doll factory in the entire world. There are others that make inexpensive dolls, jointed wooden dolls; we will not concern ourselves with these.

The dolls' heads are of porcelain bisque, and the manufacture of these heads takes on the proportions of a pottery plant. We began by going through a large shed containing a great number of tanks full of kaolin* destined to be cast into thousands of baby-doll heads. The paste taken from the tanks is kneaded, spread by rollers, and fashioned to the thickness desired, according to the size of the head to be made (there are dolls taller than a four-year-old child). Then this paste is cut into squares and placed in a mask-shaped mold. This molding is executed very quickly by women. When the heads are sufficiently firm within the molds, they take them out and dry them on boards in a special room (Fig. 1).

It is in this room that the female workers proceed with the cutting out of the eyes: they place a mold on the doll's head and cut out the opening where the glass eyes will later be fitted. Once the porcelain heads are at this stage, they must be fired like any piece of porcelain. The heads are placed one next to another on earthenware screens called *gazettes*, and these are stacked in an enormous kiln where the heads undergo firing for 27 hours.

Once this is done they are left to cool, and then each one is rubbed with sandpaper in order to give it an absolutely smooth and polished surface.

That is the first part of the process, manufacturing the porcelain, but the heads are not yet finished. We proceed into a second part of the Montreuil factory where no fewer than 350 male and female workers are employed. This is the decoration shop, or the porcelain painting workshop (Fig. 2). Each female worker, seated in front of a small workbench, has before her a series of dolls' heads, paints and brushes; her job is to paint the eyebrows of the doll; in another workshop, they paint the lips and the cheeks. It takes many coats for each shade.

When the painting is finished the heads are placed in an oven with a temperature lower than that necessary to fire the kaolin. They are baked for seven hours. The dolls' heads are then finished.

After the heads, we will describe the workshop where the eyes are made; here twenty girls are busy melting sticks of glass with a welding tool. They perform this task with great ability. There are large and small eyes, to match the size of the head and the color of the hair, because there are both blonde and brunette dolls. The eyes go to another workshop where male workers attach them with wax to the place cut out for them in the porcelain heads. In the same area a related item is manufactured, the mechanism for the movable eyelids which enables the deluxe dolls to open and close their eyes.

*Kaolin: porcelain or china clay.

The making of the doll's body is no less interesting than that of its head; this consists of a very special papier-mâché assembly. Each part of the doll's body – the bust, legs, arms and hands – is made in a cast-iron mold in which the workers place, one above the other, pieces of paper coated with paste (Fig. 3). The paper is placed in the molds with special small wooden tools, and when it is removed it has been transformed into some limb or section of the body.

When the different parts of the body are molded, they are set to dry on hurdles, then the parts are pasted together. Next the *cuvettes* are put in place. In the making of dolls, this is the name given to the small discs of metal, cardboard or wood to which are attached the rubber loops that aid in the movement of the arms and legs.

When the different parts of the body are put together, they are sent to the paint shop. A thick coat of zinc white is first applied to the body, and nothing is more amusing than to see the room where this operation is performed. Each female worker holds a large brush with which she daubs the limbs of the large and small dolls. When the legs and body are whitened, they are set to dry, then they go to other workshops where they are painted a flesh tone. Five coats of paint go on successively, then a coat of varnish is applied, and then comes the drying process as in the previous workshop.

We arrive now at the fitting, which consists of joining the separate sections and attaching them by means of the *cuvettes* and strong rubber loops that allow the limbs to move at the joints. The rubber of the legs is inserted into the thigh and is joined to the one in the middle of the body, where it is attached to an iron hook that holds the entire chest; the same applies to the forearms.

The doll is complete except for the head. A hook is adapted to the shoulders, where it is attached by means of a contrivance made from a solid wood frame (Fig. 4). This hook goes through the neck, which is screwed on in a way that allows the doll to move its head.

Nothing remains but the hair. The back of the porcelain head is provided with a piece of cork to which the locks of blonde or brunette hair are attached. The wigs also have their workshops, which are not the least curious areas of the Montreuil factory.

But it is necessary to be brief so as not to tire the patience of our readers; we will say nothing about several other workshops, particularly those where they make the "voices" of the talking dolls that say *papa* and *maman*. These involve secrets of manufacturing that we do not want to reveal indiscreetly.

Is that all? No. Here again is the large shipping room of the dolls (Fig. 5); an elegant chemise is put on each doll, and it is placed in a cardboard box, which it will not leave until greeted by the cries of joy of the "little mother" who will have the task of dressing it.

The doll factory at Montreuil was created in its entirety by Mr. Jumeau, who has completely organized it in every detail, and who has substituted a completely new industry for the production of the old leather dolls created by his father. This very extensive industry is resisting the German competition, and giving all countries of the world charming examples of the good taste of Parisian manufacturing; it thus merits the greatest praise.

During the second half of the nineteenth century, the mechanical toy or automaton had become a very popular plaything. Leading French doll firms, including Jumeau, made bisque heads to order for automaton makers. Frequently Jumeau himself purchased the working portion of

Fig. 1. Doll factory at Montreuil, near Paris. Room in which dolls' heads dry before the firing and in which the eyes are cut out.

Fig. 2. Decoration shop. Painting the dolls' heads.

Fig. 3. Shop where the parts of the dolls' bodies are molded.

Fig. 4. Doll factory at Montreuil, near Paris. Placing the porcelain heads on the dolls. (There appear to be two types of bodies on the counter: the one-piece torso and the two-piece torso which is separated at the waistline to enable a voice box to be inserted into the body. — *M.W.*)

Fig. 5. Shipping room at the Montreuil doll factory.

the performing figure and placed one of his own doll heads on it, creating a highly sophisticated group of animated figures doing such amazing things as pouring tea, blowing bubbles, playing instruments and performing magic tricks (see pages 33 to 43).

Heads with Jumeau marks have been found on automatons made by Roullet-Decamps, G. Vichy and Leopold Lambert, and keys for these figures have been found with the inititals R D and L.B. Collectors have a tendency to date the bisque-head automatons much too early; for although a great number were produced during the latter half of the nineteenth century, such firms as Decamps and Leopold Lambert carried the same models well into the twentieth century.

Thomas Alva Edison patented a mechanism for a talking doll in 1878. The Edison phonograph doll was first manufactured in 1889 in Orange, New Jersey. The success of this doll prompted Emile Jumeau to manufacture one of his own design. In 1893, he advertised a talking, singing doll that recited up to 30 words, and in 1894 he advertised an improvement which used a cylinder for changing the recitation into French, Spanish or English. People often confuse these Jumeau and Edison dolls, but they are really quite different in construction and appearance. Edison used German bisque heads, quite often marked "Simon & Halbig," whereas Jumeau used his own bisque heads which were marked "Bébé Jumeau Bte. SGDG Déposé." The Edison doll had a metal torso and wooden hands and legs which were made in the United States. The phonograph mechanism had a small wax-covered wheel which revolved on a steel rod, with one end of the rod protruding from the doll's back. When this rod was turned by a key, the doll talked. The Jumeau doll had a composition torso and arms and legs which were manufactured at the Jumeau factory. A removable metal plate in the front of the torso covered the phonograph mechanism. Changeable records with wax cylinders marked "Bébé Jumeau Phonographe" and the trademark of Lioret were placed in the torso. The record was set in motion by a clockwork mechanism wound from the back and controlled by a plunger which caused the record to play when it was pulled out and to stop when it was pushed in (see page 53).

By 1895, Jumeau and other French doll manufacturers began to feel the impact of German dolls upon the market. Labor costs were much higher in France, and Jumeau felt compelled to reduce the price of his dolls, thereby losing some of the quality he had always insisted upon. The golden age of Jumeau was over!

Several French firms attempted to save the French doll industry, and in 1899 formed a coalition or syndicate in an attempt to cut production costs and to meet German competition. The organization included the firms of Jumeau, Bru, Fleischman and Blodel, Raberty and Delphieu, and Pintel and Godshaux. These doll manufacturers became known as the Société Française de Fabrication de Bébés et Jouets, or the SFBJ.

Two daughters of Emile Jumeau served on the board of this newly formed company and were probably instrumental in keeping the Jumeau name alive—at least temporarily. All of the original Jumeau molds were saved and used by the SFBJ in limited numbers. This means that many of the Bébés often thought to date before 1900 could possibly have been made later—at least up to the time of World War I.

The SFBJ appeared to make great progress until the end of World War I, probably because there was no competition from the Germans during the war. The French, even though they were at war, still provided a market for the beautiful French dolls produced at Montreuil. This gave France a clear field in the doll industry.

By 1922 new foreign markets began to open up for the SFBJ dolls. Chocolate-colored and mulatto dolls were manufactured in large quantities to meet this foreign trade. A very strong market developed in South America and Australia. It is interesting to note that although orders from the United States increased, the French never considered the American market one of their best sources of revenue.

A story about the SFBJ factory published in 1922 in the American trade magazine *Playthings* reported that the company which employed 2800 people had produced six million dolls in 1921 and was contemplating an increase of 25% during 1922. The report also described the company's art department where clothing styles were created for the dolls under the direction of Madame Bonneaud. Her work required as much skill, artistic ability and creative talent as for the creation of the leading fashion designs of Paris. The methods used for the production of clothing for the dolls were just as efficient as for the production of clothing for human beings. Two thousand costumes were designed for the dolls in the SFBJ factory, including costumes for the so-called character dolls. In addition to the costumes, toy wardrobe trunks, which were exact replicas of real wardrobe trunks, were made.

Among the most famous dolls made by the SFBJ were the Princesses' Dolls, made in 1938 when King George VI and his wife Queen Elizabeth of England made an official visit to France. Princess Elizabeth (later Queen Elizabeth II) and her sister Princess Margaret Rose were not able to accompany their parents on this trip, and the French people, particularly the children, were very disappointed. A plan was devised to commission a pair of dolls to be made for the little princesses and to be presented to the King and Queen as a gift from the children of France.

The dolls were 32" high with bisque heads, sleeping eyes, real hair wigs and with the back of the heads incised "Unis France 306 149 Jumeau 1938." Money was raised through public contributions to create the finest wardrobes and accessories for the dolls. France's leading designers, milliners and jewelers offered their assistance. Special fabrics were woven at the famous silk mills of Lyons, and artists designed special patterns for the wardrobe. The hair styles were created by Antoine; the shoes by Hellstern, maker of ballet shoes for the Opéra Comique; toilet articles by the firm Aux Tortues (House of Tortoise Shell). Fifteen blue leather trunks, trimmed in silver, were made to hold the elaborate wardrobe.

The dolls were loaned by the Queen to the Canadian National Committee on Refugees and sent on tour in Canada to benefit European refugees and evacuees from Britain. The brochure distributed by this organization during the tour states that "Each wardrobe was planned to be the most perfect ever created for a woman and is complete to the smallest detail. Months of the most expert work, of fine embroidery and handwork went into their creation. Hundreds of Parisian seamstresses worked on them – girls who later worked on war materials in French munition plants."

One of the gowns in the collection was of special interest, and is described in the brochure: "A very old custom is symbolized by one of the lovely costumes which is tied with wheat straw. This gown is embroidered with straw which has been dyed and used as thread. Poppies, marguerites and cornflowers, the red, white and blue of the Republic, are used for trimming. During ceremonies or fêtes in rural France, bouquets of these flowers are gathered from the fields and used for decorative purposes. Visiting celebrities, even kings or diplomats, are always presented by a child with a bouquet of these same flowers mingled with ears of wheat and tied with a strand of wheat straw."

There is a misconception among many doll fanciers that these dolls were intended to represent the princesses and were named Princess Elizabeth and Princess Margaret Rose. The dolls were, in fact, named "France" for the country and "Marianne" for the Republic and the people, and are called by these names in the Canadian brochure.

Twelve sets of the 32" Princesses' Dolls were supposedly manufactured and exported to the United States. At the same time an 18" version of the two dolls was made. These are the dolls shown on page 74. No record has been found to determine how many of this smaller set were manufactured.

Although the SFBJ worked hard to compete with the German doll industry, they were not successful. By the end of the 1930's the Germans, having thrown off the effects of the war, had once again become the leaders in the doll manufacturing field. Their ability to create and manufacture dolls at much lower cost than the French brought an end to France's position as a leader in the doll industry. The SFBJ limped on for another thirty years, even surviving another world war and eventually was dissolved in 1958.

The JUMEAU DOLL

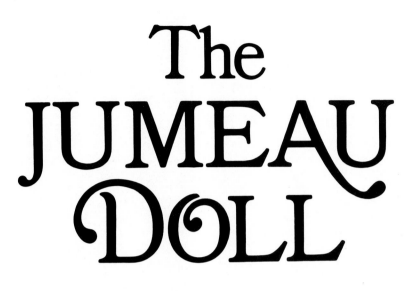

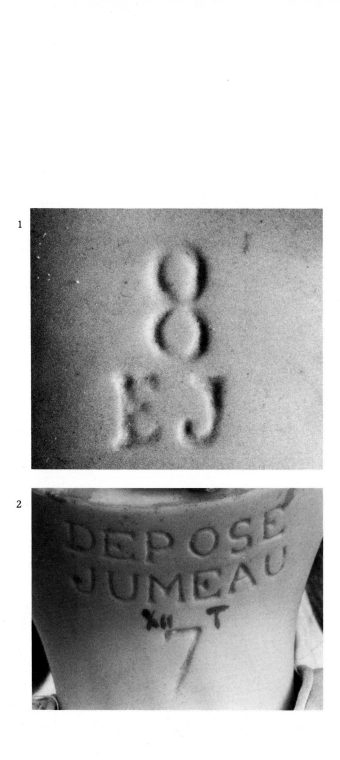

Emile Jumeau used various markings on his dolls, and these markings are especially helpful in authentication. The dolls on this spread are all marked on the backs of their heads. (1) The raised letters "EJ" and the number "8" designating the size of the head. (2) "Déposé Jumeau" incised in the bisque. (3) The mark stamped in red. (4) The incised "1907" used by the Société Française de Fabrication de Bébés et Jouets.

3

DÉPOSÉ
TÈTE JUMEAU
Bté S.G.D.G.

10

4

1907
7

Markings are also often found impressed on the soles of the shoes of Jumeau dolls. Emile Jumeau registered the "Paris Déposé" mark with the bee symbol in 1891; prior to that he used the "Bébé Jumeau" mark.

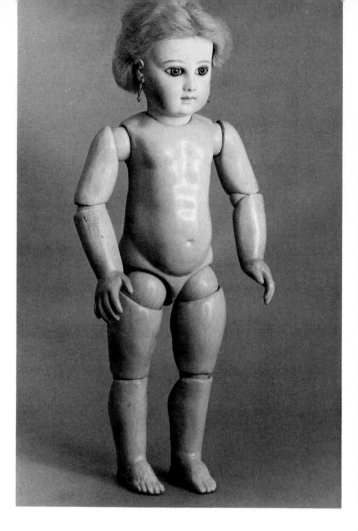

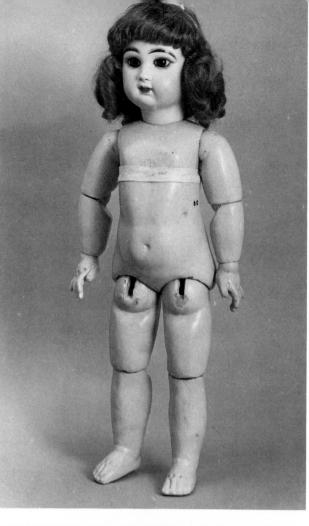

Emile Jumeau used many styles of composition jointed
bodies in his dolls. What may possibly be the earliest type
of doll, with a one-piece lower arm, is shown in the upper
left photograph. The doll in the upper right photograph –
probably a later version – has swivel joints at the wrist
and a different type of hip joint. The torso is made in two
sections, fastened together with tape. A voice box, oper-
ated by two strings protruding from the side of the doll, is
encased in the torso. The bottom photograph shows a doll
with an entirely different torso; the narrow waist and
slightly shaped bosom suggest a more mature figure.

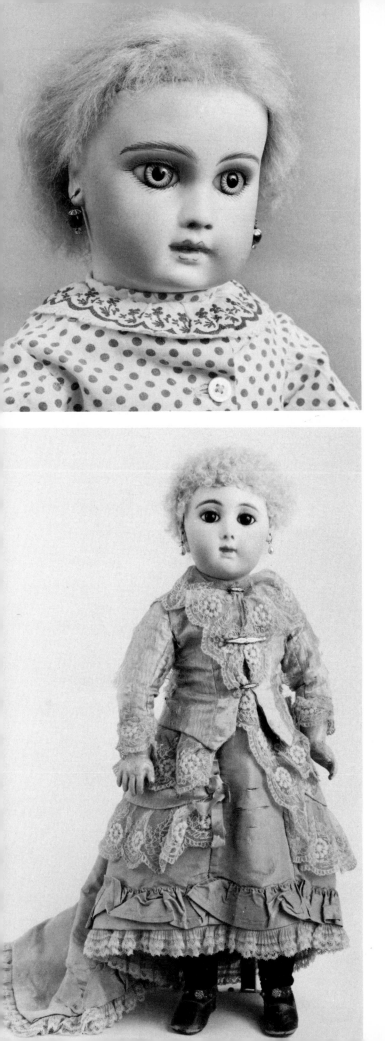

These two early unmarked dolls with bisque heads are representative of a type sometimes called a "portrait doll." Each of the dolls has a closed mouth, pierced ears and paperweight eyes. The wigs are goat skin. Both have composition jointed bodies with a one-piece lower arm and are stamped on the back "Jumeau Médaille d'Or Paris." The dolls were not necessarily intended to be "portraits" of actual persons. Paperweight eyes are those made of blown glass with the fine detail found in blown-glass paperweights.

These dolls are typical of the "long face" or "Cody" Jumeau. Both have bisque heads with no identifying marks. Supposedly these long face dolls were named after Buffalo Bill Cody who is said to have purchased such a doll when he visited France in 1889. There is no proof to indicate whether this actually occurred.

A 10″ bisque head doll with paperweight eyes, closed mouth, pierced ears and a blonde mohair wig. The back of the head is incised with the name "Jumeau" within a frame. The composition jointed body has the one-piece lower arm shown on page 19, and is stamped "Jumeau Médaille d'Or Paris."

Opposite: This 15″ lady type doll has a kid body with a slender waist shaped to accent the fit of the fashionable gown she is wearing. The doll has a swivel neck and bisque shoulder plate, large brown paperweight eyes, a closed mouth and pierced ears. The back of the head is marked with the Jumeau red check marks. The blue stamped marking on her body reads, "Jumeau Médaille d'Or Paris."

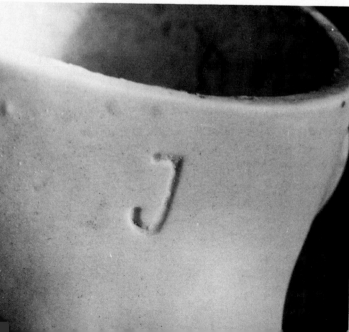

Front and back views of a 25″ bisque head doll with large paperweight eyes, pierced ears, a closed mouth and real hair wig. The back of the head is incised only with a "J." Her composition jointed body has the one-piece lower arm shown on page 19, and the back of the torso has a paper label which reads " Bébé Jumeau Diplôme d'Honneur."

Opposite: Front and back views of a 26½″ bisque head doll with large paperweight eyes, closed mouth, pierced ears and a blonde wig made of real hair. The back of the head is incised with an unusual combination of letters "CF" and "J." The "J" is the same style found on other Jumeau dolls, but it is not known what the "CF" stands for. Her composition jointed body is the usual type found on Jumeau dolls, but the stamp has been rubbed off.

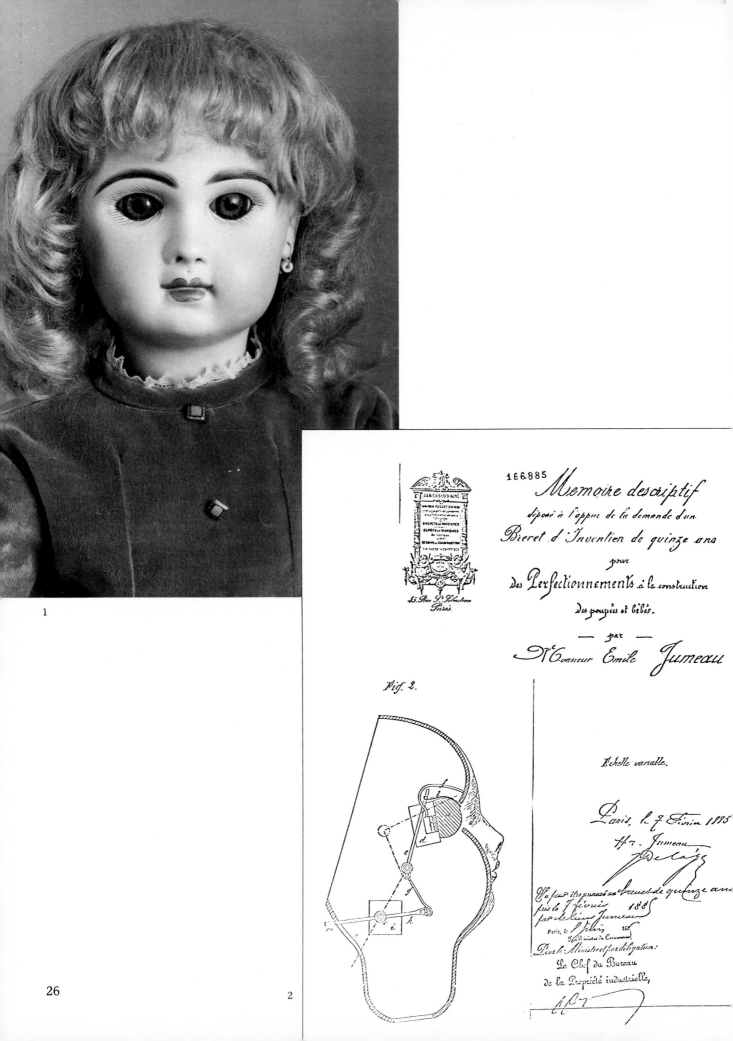

1

166.885

Mémoire descriptif
déposé à l'appui de la demande d'un
Brevet d'Invention de quinze ans
pour
des Perfectionnements à la construction
des poupées et bébés.

— par —

Monsieur Émile Jumeau

Fig. 2.

Échelle variable.

Paris, le 7 Février 1885.

26   2

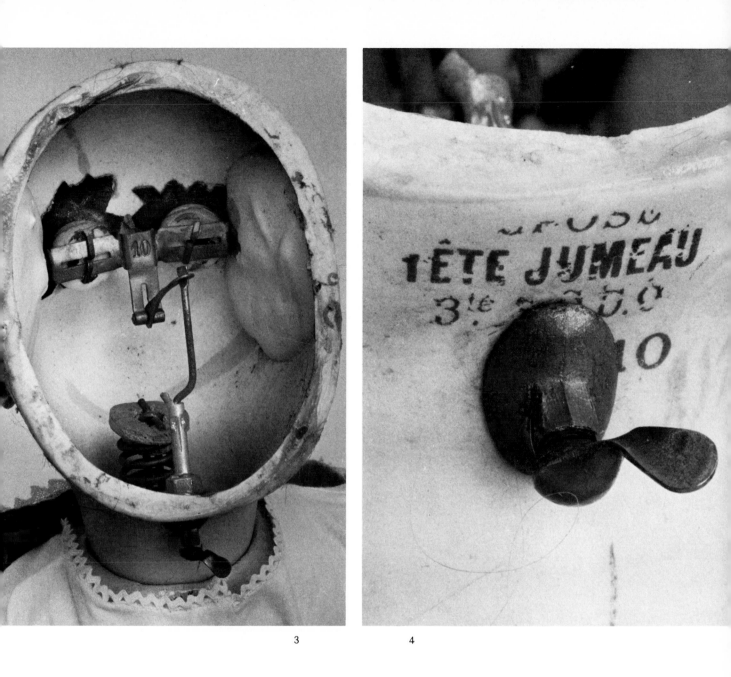

3 4

During his lifetime Emile Jumeau received a number of patents for refinements to his dolls. One of these patents, issued in 1885, covering a mechanism for opening and closing the doll's eyes, is illustrated here. (1) The doll is 22″ tall with blue glass eyes, closed mouth, pierced ears and an original blonde mohair wig. Her body is the usual composition jointed style made by Jumeau. (2) The construction drawing submitted in support of the patent application with the official grant of patent. (3) The mechanism installed in the head of the doll. (4) By turning this small metal handle at the back of the doll's head, the eyes are opened and closed. The marking above the handle, "Déposé Tête Jumeau Bte. SGDG 10," is stamped in red. The number 10, which is also incised inside the head between the eyes, signifies the size of the head.

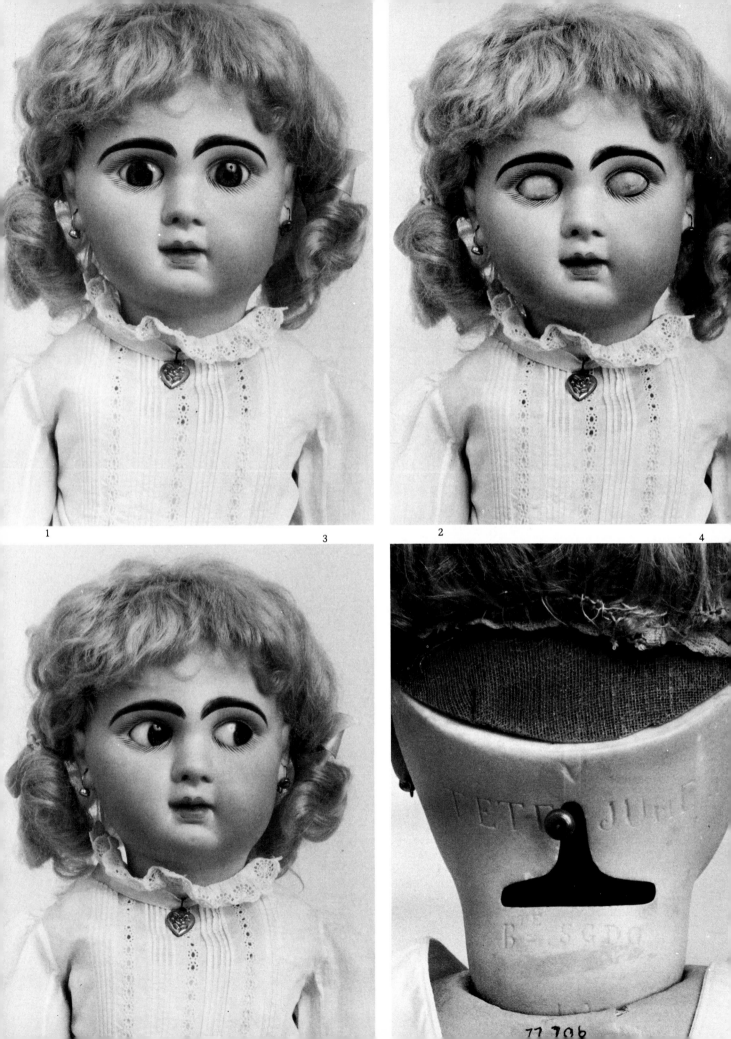

1

3

2

4

Opposite: This doll is an exceptionally rare example of one phase in Jumeau's constant striving to improve the eye movement of his doll heads. No patent has yet been found for this invention. The eyes of the doll open (1) and close (2) and also move from side to side (3). This is accomplished by a metal rod with a round ball on the end which protrudes through a "T" cut in the back of the head (4). As the rod is moved up and down or from side to side, the eyes move. The doll is 26½" tall with a bisque head, blue glass eyes, closed mouth, pierced ears and an original blonde mohair wig. The marking on the back of the head, "Tête Jumeau Bte. SGDG," is impressed in the bisque. Her body is composition and jointed throughout.

Right: It is most unusual to find a Jumeau doll such as this one, with a head made of wood. While her eyebrows and lips are crudely painted, her blue glass eyes are the beautiful paperweight French eyes one would expect to find in a Jumeau doll. Although unmarked, the body is the jointed composition type commonly found in combination with Jumeau heads. The lower picture shows a paper label with the words " Bébé Jumeau Diplôme d'Honneur" affixed to the back of the neck.

These three dolls are all in their original costumes. The doll (*left, and detail, above*) is 18½" tall with a bisque head stamped on the back with a red 7 and a check mark. Her composition jointed body has a one-piece lower arm and is stamped "Jumeau Médaille d'Or Paris."

The doll (*opposite, left*) is 21" tall with a bisque head that is stamped on the back "Déposé Tête Jumeau Bte. SGDG 9." Her composition jointed body is stamped "Jumeau Médaille d'Or Paris."

The doll (*opposite, right*) is 18" tall with a bisque head stamped "Déposé Tête Jumeau Bte. SGDG," and her composition jointed body is stamped "Jumeau Médaille d'Or Paris."

Gift of Miss Elizabeth Cheney.

The composition jointed body of this Jumeau is marked "Bébé Jumeau Bte. SGDG Déposé." She is 31" tall, has a bisque head, paperweight eyes, closed mouth and pierced ears with a real hair wig. The doll wears her original chemise with "Bébé Jumeau" stamped in gold on the ribbon band. This particular chemise appeared as late as 1919 in a Louvre store advertisement. The illustration shows the label which appeared inside the lid of the original box for this type of doll.

This doll and those pictured on the next ten pages are representatives of a type known as "musical mechanicals," in which both the music and the movement are activated by a clockwork mechanism in the doll. This 18″ doll, with bisque head and brown paperweight eyes, turns her head from side to side while fanning herself with the hand-painted fan. "Déposé Têtê Jumeau" is stamped in red on the back of the neck.

When soapy water is placed in the pewter bowl, this handsome 17½" doll raises his right hand and lowers the pipe into the bowl while bellows within the doll force bubbles through the pipe. The head is bisque with blue paperweight eyes, and "Déposé Tête Jumeau" is stamped in red on the back of the neck.

Opposite: As the music plays, this 19½" doll moves her head up and down as she raises her teapot and pours "tea" into the cup on the tray. The doll's head is bisque with beautiful brown paperweight eyes and a closed mouth. "Déposé Tête Jumeau #6" is stamped in red on the back of the neck.

Opposite: This 19½" musical mechanical doll stands at an elaborate upright piano, complete with sheet music and candelabra. When the mechanism is wound, the music plays and the doll moves her hands over the keys, turning her head from side to side and up and down. The head of the doll is made of bisque with large brown paperweight eyes and a closed mouth. The back of the neck is incised "Déposé E6J."

Right: As the music plays, the doll's head moves up and down while her left hand raises the basket lid revealing a tiny all-bisque doll inside. The entire doll is 18" tall, and her head is bisque with brown paperweight eyes and a closed mouth. "Déposé Tête Jumeau Bte. SGDG" is stamped in red on the back of the neck.

When the mechanism is wound, music plays, and the young boy moves his head up and down while his right hand pulls a string under the windmill. This string, as it is pulled down, turns the windmill. The doll is 20″ tall and has a bisque head with large blue paperweight eyes and a closed mouth. "Déposé Tête Jumeau Bte. SGDG #4" is stamped in red on the back of the neck.

Opposite: Both of these dolls have bisque heads with large paperweight eyes. As the music plays the music teacher moves her head up and down and from side to side. The baton in her right hand moves up and down in time to the music while the donkey ears on the child's hat move back and forth. The entire toy is 17½″ tall. "Déposé Tête Jumeau Bte. SGDG" is stamped in red on the teacher's head, but the head of the child bears no identifying marks.

Here is an elegant French child sitting on a basket, eating chocolate and reading a book. The doll's head turns toward the book which raises to a reading position and then lowers, while the left hand, with the piece of chocolate, raises to her mouth. The 16¼" doll has a bisque head with large blue paperweight eyes. "Déposé Tête Jumeau #4" is stamped in red on the back of the neck.

As the music plays, the doll's head moves forward so that she can look at her knitting while both hands move, simulating the motion of knitting. She is 15½″ tall and has a bisque head with large brown paperweight eyes. "Déposé Tête Jumeau Bte. SGDG" is stamped in red on the back of the neck.

Opposite: When the clockwork mechanism is wound, music plays and this doll's head swivels on her bisque shoulders, moving from side to side and up and down. She raises the flowers in her right hand, and the top of the flower basket lifts, revealing the head of a tiny doll. Both heads are of bisque; the larger doll has a very mature face with large blue paperweight eyes. The doll is 24″ tall, and "Déposé Tête Jumeau Bte. SGDG" is stamped in red on the back of the neck.

Right: When put into motion by her clockwork mechanism, this doll moves her head from side to side and up and down while her right hand raises the basket cover to reveal a small white lamb who repeatedly gives a bleating sound while turning his head. The 23½″ doll has a very mature bisque face with a swivel neck and large brown paperweight eyes. "Déposé Tête Jumeau Bte. SGDG" is stamped in red on the back of the neck.

This "long face" Jumeau (see page 21) with her original blonde mohair wig, blue paperweight eyes, applied pierced ears and closed mouth is 22" tall with an unmarked bisque head. Her composition jointed body, stamped "Jumeau Médaille d'Or," has a shaped bosom and a narrow waistline. She is dressed in a very colorful original costume with the ribbon armband lettered "Bébé Jumeau." The soles of the shoes are marked "Bébé Jumeau Med. 1878 Paris Déposé."

Pierre Jumeau called this 15″ unmarked bisque head doll a "Parisienne." Doll collectors today refer to her as a fashion doll. The head is a light chocolate color with dark brown glass eyes, a closed mouth and pierced ears. The body is made of kid, jointed at the elbows and knees, and "Jumeau Médaille d'Or Paris" is stamped on the back. She wears her original costume which probably represents a rich and distinguished woman from the Middle East.

Another French fashion doll (or Parisienne), 26" tall with a bisque head, brown paperweight eyes, a closed mouth, applied pierced ears and a real hair wig. This one has a kid body with gusset joints at the elbows and knees. The head is stamped with the red check mark attributed to Jumeau.

An unusual feature of this beauti-fully costumed 26″ bisque doll is her bisque – rather than composition – hands (see close-up below). Her original costume includes her parasol which has a molded dog's head on the handle. Her composition jointed body is marked "Jumeau Médaille d'Or Paris" on the back, and the back of the head bears the marking "Déposé Tête Jumeau 12."

This 23″ bisque head doll has blue paperweight eyes, a closed mouth and pierced ears. The back of the head bears the marking "Déposé Tête Jumeau Bte. SGDG 11," and the composition jointed body is stamped " Bébé Jumeau Bte. SGDG Déposé." She is standing in front of a doll-size American Empire dressing bureau (c. 1840) with marble columns flanking the mirror and drawers.

This 26″ bisque head Jumeau with her blue paperweight eyes, closed mouth, pierced ears and blonde real hair wig is one of the "portrait dolls." Her composition jointed body is unmarked and has the one-piece lower arm. The back of the head is incised "EJ 12."

The 17″ bisque head doll sitting on the doll-size sofa has blue paperweight eyes, an open mouth with upper teeth and a real hair wig. The back of the head is marked "Déposé Tête Jumeau 7." Her composition jointed body is stamped "Bébé Jumeau Bte. SGDG Déposé," and the soles of her shoes are marked "Paris." The sofa (c. 1835) is American mahogany Empire style, upholstered with the original horsehair fabric. The 15″ bisque head doll sitting on the floor has brown paperweight eyes, a closed mouth, pierced ears and an original blonde mohair wig. She is in her original dress and has a composition jointed body with the one-piece lower arm; the body is stamped "Jumeau Médaille d'Or Paris" on the back. The head is stamped "Déposé Tête Jumeau Bte. SGDG 5."

These twin dolls are both 15½" tall with bisque heads, blue paperweight eyes, closed mouths, pierced ears and real hair wigs. Their heads are incised "Déposé E6J," and their composition jointed bodies are stamped "Jumeau Médaille d'Or Paris."

This pair of dolls, wearing their original costumes, may have been costumed by Jumeau especially for an exhibition. Each doll is 21½″ tall with a bisque head, brown paperweight eyes, closed mouth, pierced ears and an original mohair wig. The markings on the back of their heads read "Déposé Tête Jumeau Bte. SGDG 12," and their composition jointed bodies are marked "Jumeau Médaille d'Or Paris."

Opposite: Jumeau first introduced the famous Bébé Jumeau phonograph doll in 1895. These dolls are 24″ tall and have bisque heads with paperweight eyes, pierced ears and open mouths with an upper row of teeth. The back of the heads are marked "Déposé Tête Jumeau 11," and the composition jointed bodies are stamped "Bébé Jumeau Bte. SGDG

Déposé." The doll on the right has her metal plate removed, revealing the phonograph mechanism within the torso that was set in motion by a key in the back of the doll. The label on the record reads "Bébé Jumeau Phonographe," and is marked "Polichinelle" (Punch), which indicates that the doll can say:

Bonjour, ma chère petite maman. Je suis bien sage et papa est très content. Nous irons voir Guignol pour l'entendre chanter. Pan! Pan! Qu'est-ce qu'est là? C'est Polichinelle, mamzelle. Pan! Pan! Qu'est-ce qu'est là? C'est Polichinelle, v'là. Au revoir, ma chère petite maman.

[Hello, my dear little Mommy. I am very well behaved and Daddy is so pleased. We will go to see Guignol (a puppet-show character) to hear him sing. Knock, knock. Who's there? It's Punch, Miss. Knock, knock. Who's there? It's Punch, that's who. Goodbye, my dear little Mommy!]

This 22″ bisque head doll, in her original costume, is marked "Déposé Tête Jumeau Bte. SGDG" on the back of the head. She has her original blonde mohair wig, large blue paperweight eyes, applied pierced ears, an open-closed mouth molded in a laughing position with molded white teeth. The composition jointed body is stamped "Jumeau Médaille d'Or Paris" on the back of the torso, and the soles of her shoes are marked "Bébé Jumeau Médaille d'Or Paris, Déposé."

This 26″ bisque head doll may be one that was sold with a German head and a French composition body. The head, which is unmarked, has brown glass eyes, a closed mouth and applied pierced ears. The composition jointed body is stamped "Jumeau Médaille d'Or Paris" and has the early one-piece lower arm, shown on page 19.

Opposite: These three Jumeau dolls, all in their original costumes, are standing in front of a doll-size continental china cabinet (c. 1865) made of fruitwood. The doll on the left is 17″ tall with a bisque head, blue paperweight eyes, closed mouth, applied pierced ears and a blonde real hair wig. Her head is unmarked. The composition jointed body has the one-piece lower arm (see page 19) and is stamped on the back "Jumeau Médaille d'Or Paris." The soles of the shoes are marked "Bébé Jumeau Déposé." The middle doll is 17″ tall with a bisque head, blue paperweight eyes, closed mouth, pierced ears and an original blonde mohair wig. Her composition jointed body is stamped "Jumeau Médaille d'Or Paris" and the soles of the shoes are marked "Bébé Jumeau Déposé." On the right is a bisque head doll, 19″ tall, with brown paperweight eyes, closed mouth, pierced ears and an original blonde mohair wig. Her head is marked "Déposé Tête Jumeau Bte. SGDG." Her composition jointed body has a rounded bosom, small waistline and is marked with a paper label that reads "Bébé Jumeau Diplôme d'Honneur."

Above: These three Bébé Jumeaus are all 10″ tall. The doll on the left has a bisque head with blue paperweight eyes, closed mouth, pierced ears and a real hair wig. The head is marked with the red check attributed to Jumeau. The composition jointed body has a one-piece lower arm and is stamped "Jumeau Médaille d'Or Paris." The middle doll has an unmarked bisque portrait-style head, brown paperweight eyes, closed mouth, pierced ears and her original blonde mohair wig. Her composition jointed body has the one-piece lower arm and is stamped "Jumeau Médaille d'Or Paris." Her original costume has a ribbon label sewn under the petticoat that reads "Bébé Jumeau Médaille d'Or Paris." The doll on the right has a bisque head that also bears the red check mark attributed to Jumeau, brown paperweight eyes, closed mouth, pierced ears and an original blonde mohair wig. The composition jointed body with the one-piece lower arm is stamped "Jumeau Médaille d'Or Paris."

Opposite: These four Bébé Jumeaus in their original costumes all have composition jointed bodies stamped "Jumeau Médaille d'Or Paris." They have bisque heads, paperweight eyes, closed mouths and pierced ears. They measure (*back row, left to right*) 16", 22", 19", and (*front row*) 18", and bear the following marks on their heads (*back row, left to right*): "Déposé Tête Jumeau Bte. SGDG 8"; "Déposé Tête Jumeau Bte. SGDG 10"; and a red check mark with "Jumeau" incised in the bisque; (*front row*) "Déposé Tête Jumeau Bte. SGDG 8."

Right: This 21" bisque head doll wears her original black wool wig. She is a light chocolate color with a composition jointed body and an African costume. The back of her head bears the marking "1907."

This piano-playing doll represents a much later version of the musical mechanical type shown on pages 33–43. When the clockwork mechanism is wound, the doll raises her head up and down and moves her hands over the keyboard. The doll is 13″ tall with a bisque head; "SFBJ Paris" is incised on the back of the neck.

Opposite: Sold in the 1940's by the Franz Carl Weber Toy Store in Zurich, Switzerland, all of these 10″ bisque head dolls were advertised as late as 1952. Each doll in the group has a composition body—jointed at the neck, arms and legs—and carries a gold paper identification tag which reads "Fabrication// Jumeau// Paris// Made in France." The doll in the back represents Mme. de Pompadour. In the next row are the Empress Josephine (*left*) and Queen Marie Antoinette. Left to right in the front row are the Empress Marie Louise, Sarah Bernhardt and Mme. de Sévigné. Each doll has a gold metal stand with a protruding rod which is inserted into the sole of the doll's foot.

Opposite: This group of late Jumeau dolls is much inferior to the lovely dolls made by Jumeau before 1900. At the left in the back row, is a 20″ bisque head doll with brown glass, flirty eyes, closed mouth, pierced ears and an incised mark in the back of the head which reads "Unis France 306 Jumeau 1938 Paris." The body is composition with jointed limbs. Next to her is a 20½″ pressed-cardboard-head doll with blue sleeping eyes, open mouth with teeth and an original blonde synthetic wig. The head is incised "Unis Paris 301." The body is a composition jointed style with the original costume and a paper label which reads "Fabrication Jumeau Paris Made in France." The 18½″ doll on the right in the back row, has a pressed-cardboard head with sleeping blue eyes, closed mouth and brown mohair wig. The back of the head has raised lettering which reads "Jumeau 319/6½." She also has the composition jointed

body. In the front row, on the left, is a 16½″ pressed-cardboard-head doll which is incised "Paris 301." She has blue sleeping eyes, a closed mouth and a brown synthetic wig. The composition jointed body is unmarked, but her original costume bears a paper label that reads "Bébé Français Fabrication Jumeau Paris." The 16″ doll on the right has a pressed-cardboard head with the incised mark "Paris 301," blue sleeping eyes, closed mouth and a brown synthetic wig. Her body is the composition jointed style, and the costume is original. A paper label on the dress reads "Poupée Jumeau Paris Made in France."

Above: Two short story booklets which were used by Jumeau as advertising devices. A booklet was packaged inside each doll box before shipment to America (see page 8).

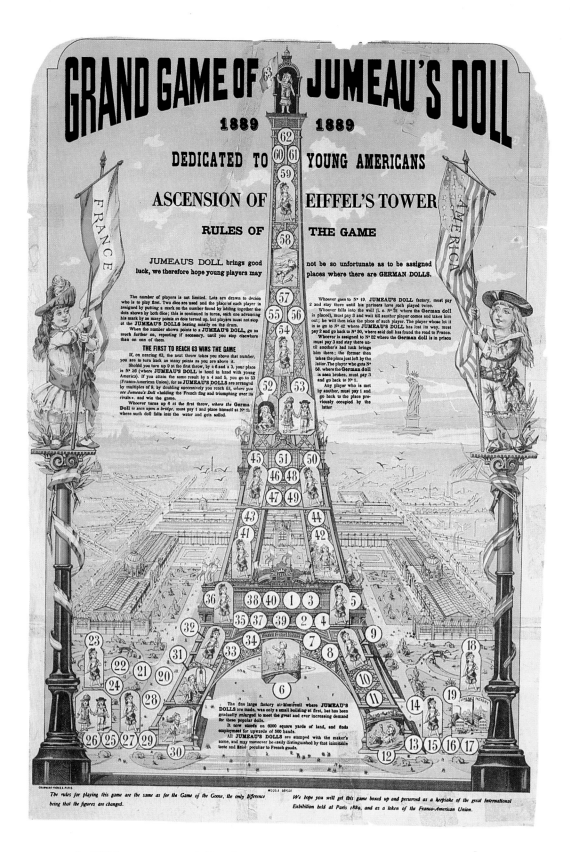

In 1889 Jumeau wrapped this sales-propaganda game around his new dolls before they were placed in boxes for shipment to America. The idea of the game was to get to the top of the Eiffel Tower, where a lovely Jumeau doll is standing, without falling on any number that represented supposedly inferior German dolls. The game's rules are patterned after the famous game "The Goose." Printed on very thin paper and intended as a throw-away, very few copies of this piece of advertising literature survive today.

This bisque head doll is marked "Déposé Tête Jumeau Bte. SGDG" on the back of the head. The doll measures 17" high and has the typical paperweight eyes, closed mouth and pierced ears with a real hair wig. Her composition body has a paper label that reads "Bébé Jumeau Diplôme d'Honneur." The original chemise is worn with a ribbon label marked "Bébé Jumeau." Her original box contains two labels on the inside; one (*above, top*) tells about the doll, and the other (*above, bottom*) shows and describes the shoes worn by the doll.

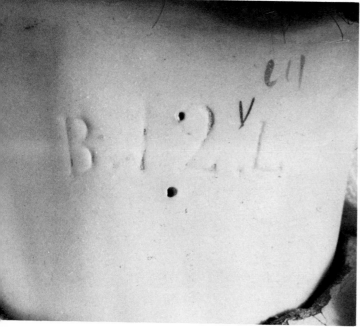

Dolls marked "BL" are probably those made especially by Emile Jumeau for the Louvre store. The two pictured here have bisque heads with the typical French eyes and both are incised "BL" with the red check marks attributed to Jumeau. The original date for these dolls has not been established, but the 1919 Louvre catalog, pictured opposite, shows one, indicating that these were made as late as 1919.

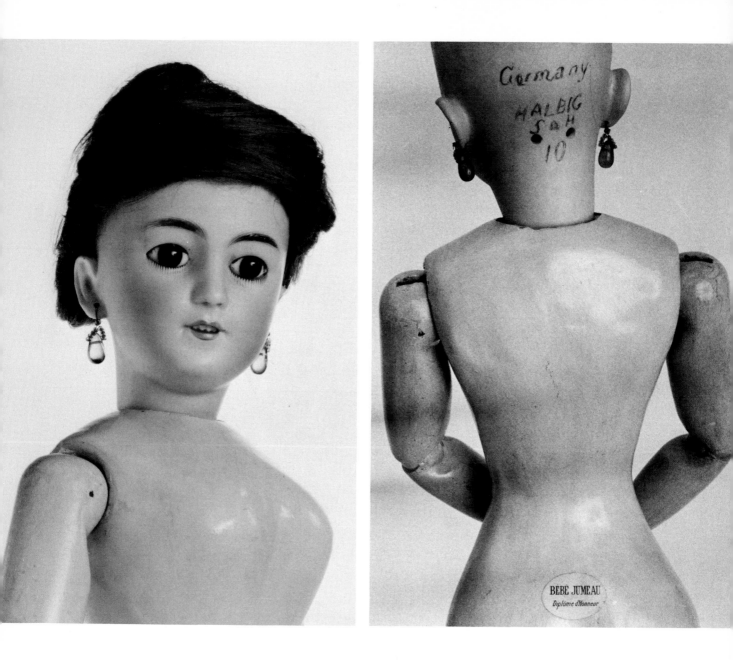

The combination of a German head, such as this one by Simon & Halbig, and a Jumeau body was not rare. This bisque head, marked "Germany Halbig S & H 10," has a longer and more mature face than what is usually seen on Jumeau dolls. The composition jointed body with its small, narrow "lady type" waistline is marked with a paper label which reads "Bébé Jumeau Diplôme d'Honneur." The doll is 22" high.

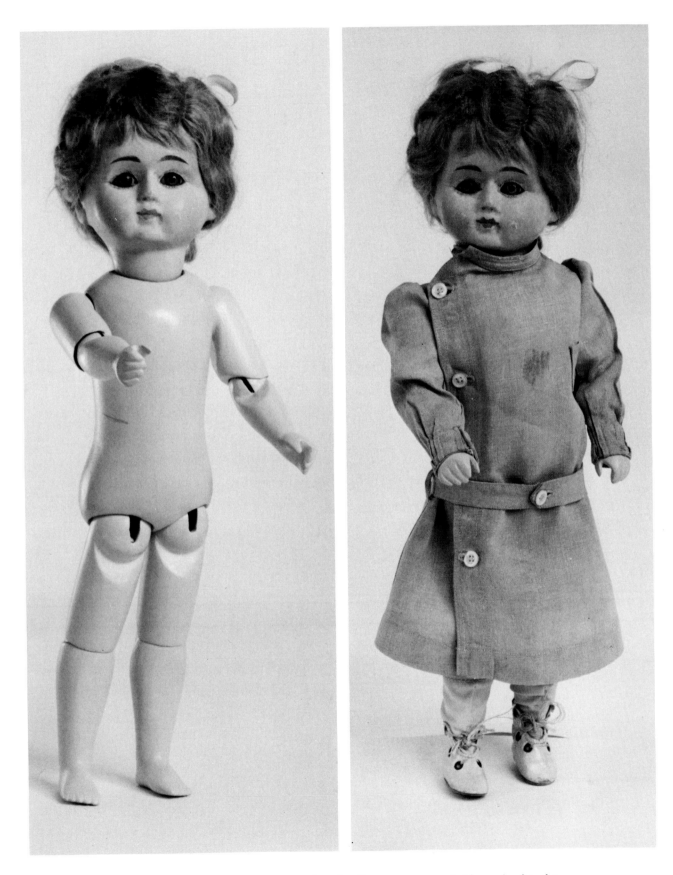

Wooden dolls such as this one, attributed to Jumeau, were probably made after the formation of the Société Française de Fabrication de Bébés et Jouets. She is jointed at the neck, shoulders, elbows, thighs and knees, and stands 13″ high.

This 11½" bisque head late Jumeau doll has a very dark complexion, and the bisque is coarse. The back of the head is incised "Unis France." She has sleeping blue eyes with an open mouth, and the paper label on her skirt reads "Poupée Jumeau Paris."

Jumeau dolls such as this one were sometimes costumed in French Provincial dress. This 8″ high bisque head doll has blue glass eyes and an open mouth. The back of the head is incised "Unis France." Her body is the composition jointed style, and the paper label on her apron reads "Exposition International Bébé Jumeau Paris 1931."

An example of a late Jumeau, this 20½" bisque head doll is made of a highly colored bisque, not the smooth pale bisque of early Jumeau dolls. The head is incised "Unis France 71 306 149 Jumeau 1938 Paris." Her body is the jointed composition "lady style" with a shaped bosom and small waist.

Opposite: One of a group of bisque head dolls sold in the 1940's by the Franz Carl Weber Toy Store in Zurich, Switzerland, this 10" doll has a composition body. The paper tag on her gown reads "fabrication Jumeau Paris Made in France." The doll represents Queen Victoria.

The Princesses' Dolls were made in 1938 to be presented by the children of France to Princess Elizabeth (later Queen Elizabeth II) and Princess Margaret Rose (see page 13). The original dolls were 32" high, and after the presentation the same dolls were made in a smaller, 18", size. The dolls pictured here are the smaller version. Both have bisque heads, a rather pink complexion, sleeping glass eyes, real hair wigs and are in their original dresses. The backs of the heads are incised "Unis France 306 149 Jumeau 1938."

Opposite: Postcards which were sold in Canada when the Princesses' Dolls were exhibited to benefit the Canadian National Committee on Refugees.

Dating Jumeau Dolls

One of the most frustrating elements in researching Jumeau dolls is dating them. Just when you feel that you can make a concrete decision about a date, something comes along that throws your firm beliefs right out the window. Because very little has been found that specifically says "Such-and-such a doll was made in this time," many of our dates are educated guesses. It is for this reason that very few dolls in this book have been given specific dates.

There are some definite criteria that are acceptable for dating Jumeau dolls:

1. A doll that has been in a family for many years with the true provenance which includes the date of purchase.
2. A doll with its original tags giving the date of purchase.
3. Advertising information, such as the booklets sold with the dolls, sometimes gives a date.
4. Matching a doll to a dated advertisement by a Paris store showing examples of and naming the current popular dolls.
5. Original boxes occasionally carry dated information on the outside.
6. Markings with dates such as "1907" or "1938" are probably the years that the dolls were made.

There are also a number of clues which can aid in placing the doll in a particular time slot:

1. Patent papers and trademarks will give you a starting date. For example: Emile Jumeau registered his trademarks "Bébé Jumeau" and "Bébé Prodige" in 1886. In 1891 he registered the "Paris Déposé" mark with a bee symbol on the soles of the dolls' shoes. In 1895 he patented the "Bébé Phonographe" and "Bébé Marcheur," and in 1896 he registered the name "Bébé Français."
2. Original costumes will show the period of the doll. Many of the "fashion dolls" were clothed in the latest Paris fashions.

3. Exposition reports give clues as to the type or types of new dolls shown at that time.
4. Buffalo Bill supposedly purchased the "long face" Jumeau in 1889.
5. Information gained from early writings about visits to the Jumeau doll factory can often help to date a doll. The pictures which accompany the 1888 Tissandier article in *La Nature* (see page 12) show dolls that appear to have the lower arms and hands in one piece. Léo Claretie mentions that in his visit to the Jumeau factory in 1894 the molds of the hands are separate, so swivel wrists are in evidence. He also mentions that the eyes are controlled by a rod which exists at the base of the neck and which can be controlled from outside the head. "The eye follows the hand and can have four movements, raised upward, lowered, and turned sideways to the left and to the right." Griffith's "A Village of Dollmakers," written in 1897, mentions that the larger dolls have the ears applied; the smaller sizes are molded with the heads. Griffith also mentions movable eyes with four movements, teeth, and the hands made separately from the arm. He also talks about the name of the maker being "branded" on the backs of the dolls before they are taken to the shoemaker.

There are also some pitfalls to beware of when attempting to date dolls:

1. A doll marked "Médaille d'Or 1878," was not necessarily made in that year. Jumeau used this mark for many years after 1878.
2. The "Unis France" mark which was first used in 1922 by the SFBJ was probably used by them until the firm went out of business.

Perhaps in the future new evidence will be uncovered, probably in the form of catalogs, that will give us all the answers.

Exposition Awards Given to Pierre & Emile Jumeau

1844   Paris, Honorable Mention
1849   Paris, Bronze Medal
1851   London, First Prize
1855   Paris, Silver Medal
1867   Paris, Silver Medal
1873   Vienna, Gold Medal and Medal of Progress
1876   Philadelphia, Gold Medal
1878   Paris, Gold Medal
1879   Sydney, Australia, Gold Medal
1880   Melbourne, Australia, Gold Medal
1884   New Orleans, Gold Medal
1885   Antwerp, Belgium, Diploma of Honor
1885   Paris, Gold Medal

Bibliography

Claretie, Léo. *Les Jouets, Histoire Fabrication*. Paris: Ancienne Maison Quantin, 1898.

Coleman, Dorothy S., Elizabeth A., and Evelyn J. *The Collector's Encyclopedia of Dolls*. New York: Crown Publishers, Inc., 1975.

– – –. *The Collector's Book of Dolls' Clothes*. New York: Crown Publishers, Inc., 1975.

Davies, Nina. *The Jumeau Doll Story*. New Orleans: Nina S. Davies, 1957.

Doll Collector's Manual. Boston: The Doll Collectors of America, 1967.

Griffith, M. Dinorben. "A Village of Dollmakers." *Pearson's Magazine*, July 1897.

Hart, Luella. *Complete French Doll Directory*. 1965.

Hillier, Mary. *Automata and Mechanical Toys*. London: Jupiter Books Limited, 1976.

Johl, Janet. *The Fascinating Story of Dolls*. New York: H. L. Lindquist Publications, 1941.

– – –. *Your Dolls and Mine*. New York: H. L. Lindquist Publications, 1952.

King, Constance Eileen. *The Collector's History of Dolls*. London: Robert Hale Limited, 1977.

Playthings. September, 1922, Vol. 20., No. 9.

St. George, Eleanor. *Dolls of Three Centuries*. New York: Charles Scribner's Sons, 1951.

Tissandier, Gaston. "The Parisian Industries, a Doll Factory." *La Nature*, 1888.